On The Shore Again

Natalie Wilde

Presentation by *BookLeaf Publishing*

Web: www.bookleafpub.com

E-mail: info@bookleafpub.com

ISBN: 9789357740074

First edition 2023

Dedicated to introverts, witches, over-thinkers, dreamers and the soft and sensitive types. We GOT this.

ACKNOWLEDGEMENT

I want to thank my mum for making me the creative person that I am.

PREFACE

This book was created for a 21 day poetry challenge. It was something I chose to take part in as it had been a while since I had written lyrics and I missed being able to express how I was feeling through words. I hope that within this collection of poems you find something you can connect with and maybe feel less alone.

THE NOW

I stepped into the moment,
Fully, Completely,
Sensed sadness surround me,
Shift inside me,
Separate, divide, fall apart,
Slip away... Melt away...

COCOON

I'm ready to unfurl my wings,
Feel my petals spreading out,
Allowing sunshine to enter in,
I've already let spring get away,
Now's my last chance to escape,
Before this place where I've come to feel safe,
Will only cause me pain.

UNRAVEL

I will not unravel.
And give it all away - this time.
The air is heavy, the darkness is beating,
Buck moon is high on the shelf,
The conditions are ripe, red dress in July,
And though I do long, to come undone,
I'm keeping me all to myself.

THE LAKE

My cheeks may stain with eager blossom, and,
My bones may ache in the ominous sun,
Blanket my body, smothered in longing,
For something unknown but never gone,
My form may dismantle with the dying leaves,
and,
My face may be stunned by the shock of frost,
Cracked and jagged lethal to touch,
Heartache, betrayal, sudden loss,
Laughter, and love, and inner peace,
Life moves in circles; things will repeat,
But I am not the ever-changing surface,
I am the stillness beneath.

WHEN I WAS READY

5

Tears in my eyes, I let you go free,
Safe in a bottle, I sent you out to sea,
Present on the beach, I stayed,
Pulling out all my vines and weeds,
And when I was ready you came back to me.

A SEPTEMBER STORY

Crescent moon, September's night,
Taking me down, the harbour side,
Tarot cards, and local bars,
Bitter beers, on haunted steps,
So many here, have laughed and left.

Red silk sheets and peppermint tea,
He's sitting in my room, playing my guitar,
The same one I'll write on, when he breaks my
heart.

And for the first time, we're crossing a line,
We're not lovers, but more than friends,
And I thought that I, could just get up and say
goodbye,
But this is how the story ends.

BETWEEN MY FINGERTIPS

I carry the Earth's weight in my heart,
Mother nature's sorrow deep inside my chest,
I sense her heavy heart with each breath I take,
The pain of every creature lost, and every fallen tree,
I try to make changes but there's an itch under my skin,
All of it feels futile against the darkness' grin,
Like a solar eclipse, I know the end is coming,
Yet I'm completely helpless, watching it unfold,
I can feel her dying, and the Earth is gently slipping,
Between my finger tips, like a river running.

THE RED OF A STRAWBERRY

The red of a strawberry glinting in the sun,
How everything falls into place when you put
the kettle on,
The wonder of the sky at night, reminding me
why I'm alive,
And when it's hot in mid July, bathing in the full
moon light
Ocean waves bursting through my feet,
A black cat in the street befriending me,
Watching Fellowship with Mum,
And in the car singing along to Bob,
Certain lines that always make us laugh,
Like the vandals with the handles, and the
potatoes to be mashed,
The bats outside my window, fluttering around
in circles,
Dancing in the evening air, against the sunset
skyline,
The smell of cut grass or chocolate cake with
icing,
Fresh sheets in the night, when a storm outside
is biting,
Going out in my favourite black dress, feeling
like a little witch,

Painting alone with a podcast on,
Dancing round my room to my favourite Taylor
song,
Reading a book in the arms of the sun, cradling
tea on the kitchen floor,
I could go on, and on, and on,
But you asked if I was scared to lose you and
this is my reply,
The things you love make you who you are,
And if you ever leave I've still got plenty more.

ATROPA BELLADONNA

She used to think that being pretty, was the key
to being happy, so she planned to save up her
money, dye her hair and change her face. But
forget about all of that right now, you're worried
about your future and there's a fair in town, so
you stumble on over to the fortune teller, with a
fistful of hope and a couple of dollars. Inside a
dream, you see a girl, with ebony hair and a
berry red smile - (she looks a lot like the ideal
you) - an Atropa Belladonna, on a vine,
beautiful and mysterious, glinting in the sun,
under the surface is something much more
ominous, not maleficent or evil, but broken and
bleeding - a depressed form of poisonous -
leaking black and blue ink as she weeps and if
you could hear her speak she'd say... "Don't you
know who I am? I'm the saddest girl that you
have ever met, why don't you take a look? And
come on, come on, come on girl, tell me, tell me,
tell me now, wouldn't you wanna be just like
me?"...
Because roses are still vulnerable to the drying
heat,
Berries will be picked and discarded once more,
The oceans are tainted with nonchalance,

And crystals will be left to fade in the sun,
And if you were beautiful would you even know
it?
And if you are beautiful do you even know it?

She used to think that being pretty, was the key
to being happy.

LONGING IN THE NIGHT

She's not good at getting near,
She flies to the flame, then disappears,
A night jar close to her sings his midnight tune,
She knows he wants to take her heart and paint it
maroon,
Well sorry honey she's too busy falling for the
moon,
And she wishes her heart could just be still,
But it dances like a flame on a breezy hill,

Well I guess it must be true,
We always want what we can't have,

But he fights against the dark and he owns the
biggest star,
He's painted in the sky like a work of art,
He doesn't need her; he's loved by the world,
Just like the moon, he's just like the moon,
So out of reach, he's so out of reach.

POEM BY AN ANNOYING VEGAN (SORRY)

It's 40 degrees in mid July and the grass in
London's perished,
And they'll complain and put it on the news and
write articles all about it,
Yet everywhere I turn it seems nobody cares…
Streets, seas and beaches, infected with plastic
poison,
Creatures we claim to love on the edge of
extinction,
Calves and lambs snatched from their mothers,
The air is cursed with disease and sulphur,
The forests are burning and quickly fading,
And we stand back and watch as the creatures
suffer,
Yet they won't take their litter home; it's easier
to fling it,
They'll never give up meat; it just "tastes too
good to eat it",
Fast fashion's just too cheap and easy, and "it's
always been done this way".
After all were "top of the food chain",
And god forbid wind turbines make the
landscape look ugly!,

Well I guess it's easier to ignore it, and I'm not
saying that I'm perfect, (definitely not! - I
sometimes still eat chocolate),
But I've tried so hard to understand it, and I've
tried to be empathetic,
But when we all burn with the Earth,
Well then I guess we were asking for it.

WITCHY LOVE

Her hair is an onyx black river of wonder,
Flowing free in rivulets, twisting in the breeze,
Her skin is porcelain delicate, glistening like the
moon,
Her cheeks are white roses, pinched with berry
kiss,
Her lips are strawberries, freshly picked,
Oozing nature's sweetness,
Her movements are soft and graceful,
As she moves through the air,
Limbs elegantly tracing, the surface of the dirt,
She worships the moon and prays to the sun,
She is a witch, a pagan woman, one of nature's
children,
She is the whisper in the wind,
The embers of the fire,
She is the subtle shift in Spring,
And when the nights get darker,
She is the flicker of the candle,
And the darkness framing,
She'll love you 'til her breathing stops,
And love you like a forest fire,
But you can never contain her,
And you will never own her,

A part of her will always dance, to the rhythm of nature.

I DRANK TOO MUCH

I don't think I really want to die,
Maybe only sometimes,
I probably just drank too much,
My demons don't drown they float and pop, and
come spilling out the top,
I can't control them when I'm laced with poison,
And I'm so tired of pulling on their leash,
So I let them overspill, corrupting the world
around me,
A crushing wave of thoughts and grief,
Maybe if yours sense them, our demons will be
friends,
And I'll wear them like a painting, and pretend
they make me different,
Or maybe I'll say too much - or worse - tears
overflow into my cup,
But either way I'm paying the price, waking in
the morning,
Scurrying around, picking them back up, ever
so quietly,
See now they're dripping and loaded, full of
anxiety…

MORNING MOON

I woke up at six thirty with sludge in my chest,
And stumbled out of bed,
Dreading a day of more of the same,
With this greyness stuck in my head.

I dragged back the curtain and to my surprise,
Found a snow moon pinned between trees,
Glorious and golden against a purple pink sky,
And morning birds rejoicing beneath.

And for a split second I could taste the lie,
As colour came back to my life,
Rivers can flow when you just exist,
How I could I forget? Go unconscious again?
I'm thankful for moments like this.

INTROVERT

I know that you think that you're better than me,
'Cause I've got too many thoughts in my head,
But I've got my lyrics, my paints and my music,
I'll live on as art when we're dead.

FOREST WITCH

She lived in a city that fed off of stories, of the
lonesome and empty,
The energy was impatient and the nights
unsteady,
And though the rain was heavy, the sadness
foamed and bubbled right up,
It spread to the corners and down the dark
alleys,
Until everyone was all for oneself,
She lived there 'til she could no longer bear it,
And made a plan to somehow escape it,
To somewhere that was home, but what was
home? - she did not know,
She searched the world over 'til she happened
upon a forest,
With a nurturing darkness, a loving embrace,
She immersed her brokenness in the space
between trees,
Emptied her tears into the lakes and streams,
Buried her eager heart in the undergrowth,
And screamed to the moon 'til her lungs opened
up,
And when she could breathe again she arose,
Her hands were steady, and a stillness flowed,
out from her darkest depths within,

It was then that she knew home had always been
inside her,
The forest just helped her to find her.

LILITH

I hear myself singing Graceland Too,
Standing in the kitchen, waiting for you,
"Whatever she wants" and whatever she needs,
Sweet melody's threading me to you,

Standing on a balcony, overlooking the view,
Terracotta rooftops and ocean peeking through,
My arms hold you safe, white bonnet frames
your face,
Bright eyes sparkle out underneath,

Midday, I'm working, city outside is humming,
But here we are safe in this plant flowing place,
Pumpkin is purring, you discover his shape,
Then grin up at me with paint on your face,

The noises excite you, standing in the crowd,
It's our favourite place, looking up at the stage,
Promised that I'd take you, eight candles on
your cake,
You've got your favourite dress on, tutu glitter
grey,

Autumn cold, your hair is stained darker,
Trip home, you thought you'd drop by,

Hot tea on the table, catching up on laughter,
An October storm seeking outside,

I saw you so clearly in my mind,
Mirrors of me but a beautiful kind,
A Wednesday, a Lilith, a cat in the night,
Budding with joy and a love for life,
Swore I'd protect you to my last breath,
But you can't protect someone you've never
met.

No sound could be found when he severed the
thread,
Gold and pink faded, to black and bled,
Watched it all burn to the ground,
Watched the dream as it floated out,
Standing on the shore again I knew,
When I lost him I lost you too.

RED STRING OF FATE

I will wait 'til I feel no tugs,
To follow a different direction,
I trust the ribbon to lead me out,
Leaving all the wrong faces, lying in my wake,
Tangled up with time, learning from mistakes,
Side stepping erroneous embraces,
A flash of red, a sense of peace,
Signs and synchronicities,
And I'm sure I'll know when the time has come,
When I remember you all along.

LOVE AND LUST AND DUST

You are like sunshine,
I wish to bottle you up,
Even when you are far, I sense your touch
I long to dip my fingers inside your fire,
Dance with you upon my funeral pyre,
I'll watch as your flame soaks me up,
Until there's nothing left of me but dust,
Even then you still wouldn't be close enough.

DAYLIGHT

I can't believe I've been asleep, my whole life,
Trapped inside my own dark shadow,
Living in black and white,
I thought I'd be sad forever,
But something inside me has changed,
Now I know the lie.

I found that love has many colours,
Pink and gold, the strongest,
I learned it's always best to let go,
The nights I don't are the longest,
And never seek external forms, looking for the
sun,
Sunshine will only ever come, when it flows
within,
I thought I'd be sad forever,
In the upside down, stuck in a twilight,
But something inside me has changed,
Now I only see the Daylight.

WHEN IT IS OVER

When it is over, I find myself in the desert,
Each step I take greets me with death,
Though there is space to run - I'm confined,
As the forests inside me gasp for breath,
I feel my hunger and craving, to turn back to
who I was before;
I can't, the page has turned,
I must return to the shore, before I merge with
the sun,
Her rage destroying what is left of the trees,
Now looking at the sand between my toes, I
must decide to wade right in,
To the ocean's darkest depths, and take the first
step,
I become one with her, let her engulf me, take
me under,
Bathe the cuts and wounds; give them space to
hurt,
And when it is over, she hands me back to the
beach,
And I retreat from the shore once again.

www.ingramcontent.com/pod-product-compliance
Lightning Source LLC
LaVergne TN
LVHW010843200726

843508LV00012B/2731